THIS BOOK
BELONGS TO

COLOR TESTE

COOKING

Rain

SINGING

DRAIVING

Dance

BOOKS

SLEEP

SHOPPING

MESSAGE

WRITE

Read

Gym

TREE

Fall

SPRING

Sun

FLY

LISTENING

STAR

MOTH

FRIENDS

NIGHT

CHRISTMAS

KITTEN

Space

SPACESHIP

FLOWER

DONUT

Balloon

SHOWER

HELLO

WIZARD

Romance

Toys

DESK LAMP

CUTe

Lovely

Zen Caticorn

PIRAT CATICORN

PIZZACATICORN

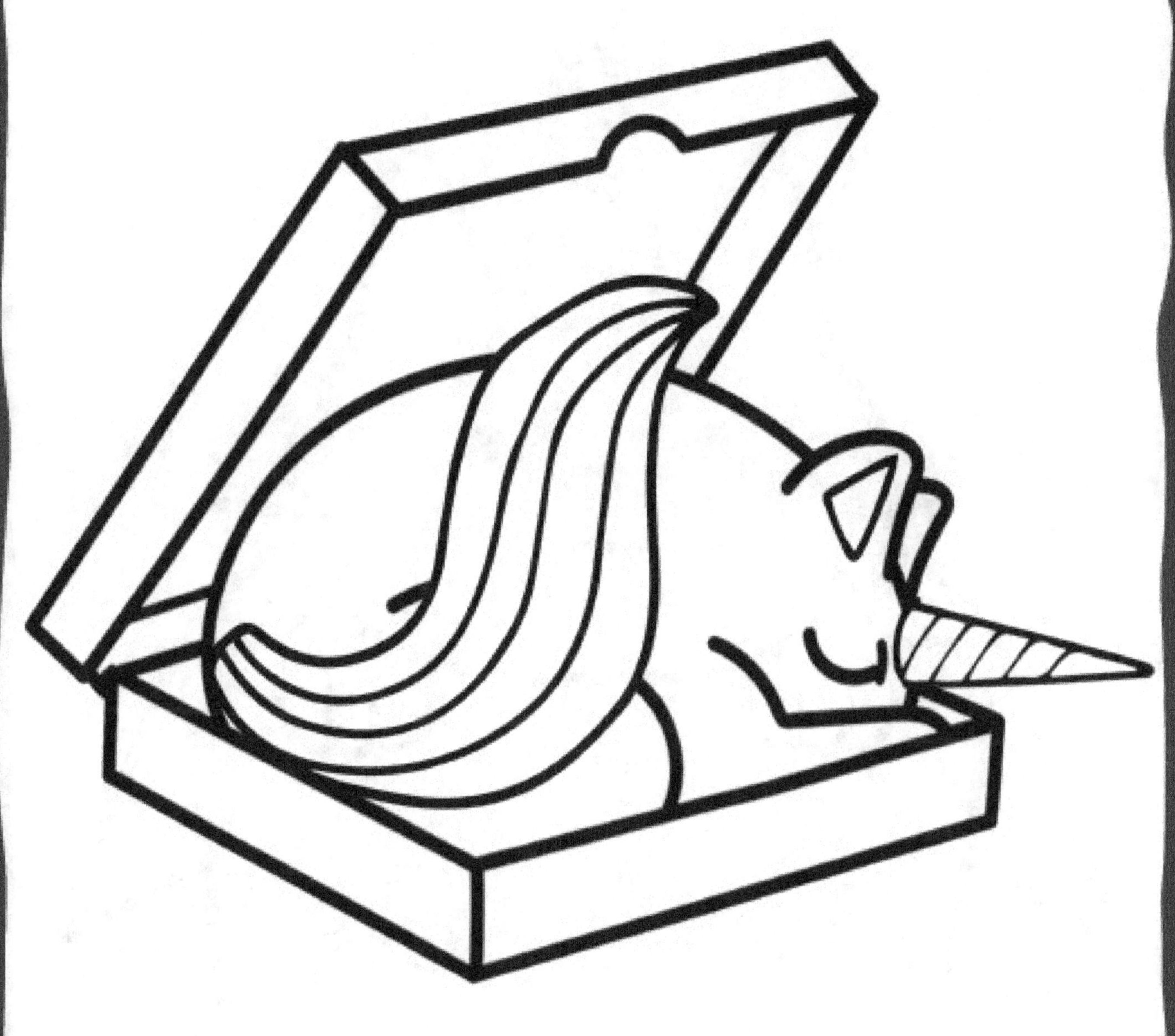

BOX

House